BEVERLY MASSACHUSETTS

DESIGN PARTS SOURCEBOOK

Romantic

ROCKPORT PUBLISHERS

MdN DESIGNS

First published in the United States of America by
Rockport Publishers, a member of
Quayside Publishing Group
100 Cummings Center
Suite 406-L
Beverly, Massachusetts 01915-6101
Telephone: (978) 282-9590
Fax: (978) 283-2742
www.rockpub.com

ISBN-13: 978-1-59253-500-2
ISBN-10: 1-59253-500-3

10 9 8 7 6 5 4 3 2 1

Book design for English version: Chie Arakawa

Printed in Singapore

Romantic: A state of being sentimental, sweet, and away from real life.
A tendency to be fond of these thoughts and feelings. A state of being fanciful.

— *From Daijisen*

All those roses, lace, rabbits, embroidery
— they are sweet, heartwarming, and tender
— look as if they slipped out of foreign children's stories.
It's a new world made with dreamy parts.

They are new, though they have not changed from the old days.
They look elegant, though they have natural taste.
Such a mixture of wonder is romantic.

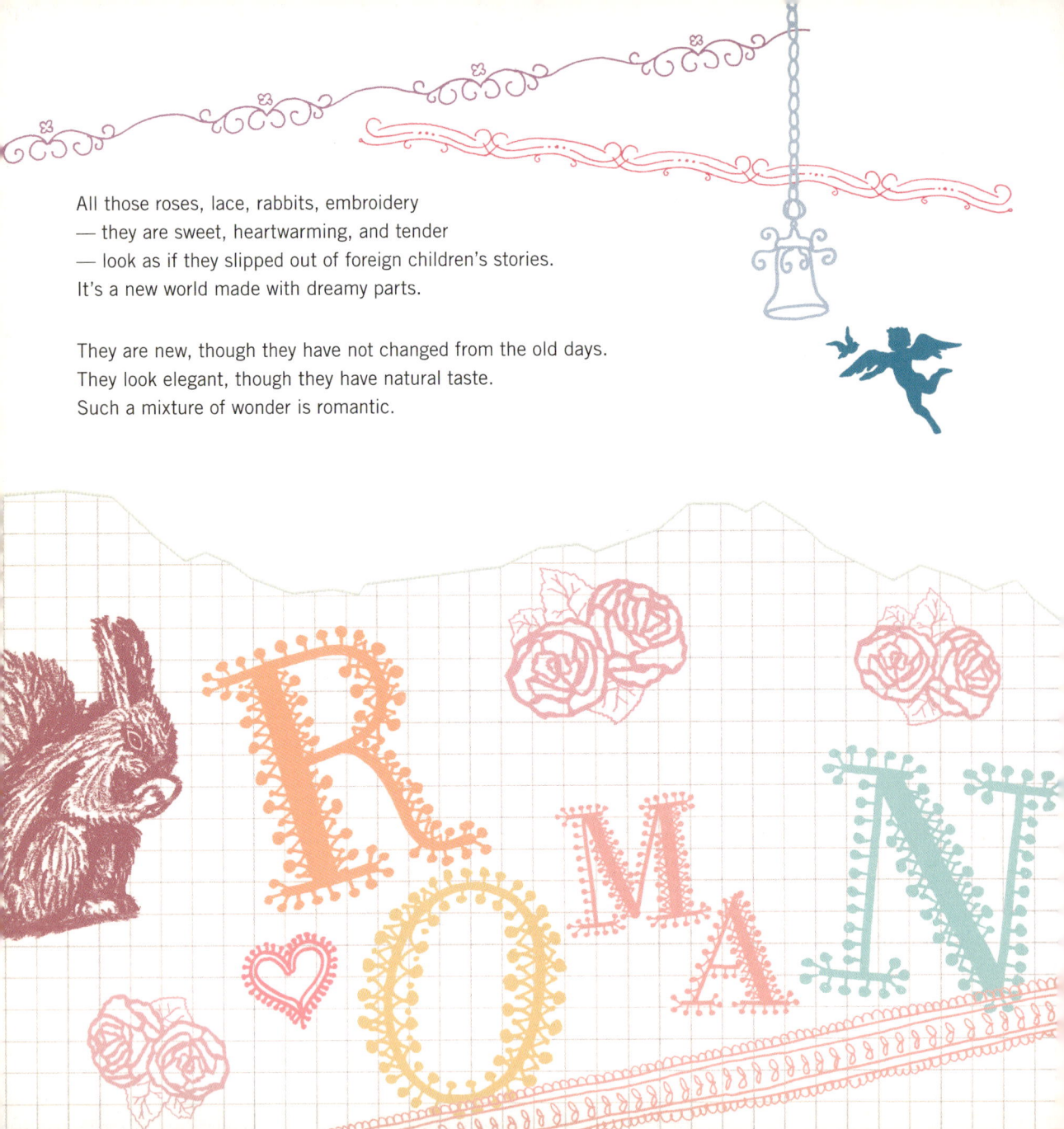

CONTENTS

FLOWER
42 parts
p 008

GREEN
59 parts
p 012

ANIMAL
44 parts
p 018

GOODS
60 parts
p 022

LINE
32 parts
p 030

CORNER
64 parts
p 042

RIBBON
36 parts
p 036

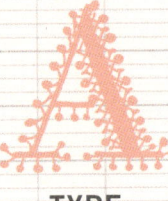

TYPE
248 parts
p 058

FLAME
47 parts
p 050

The background material on this page is paper10 (p 104).

LACE
6 parts

p 070

FEATHER
11 parts

p 072

PAINT
16 parts

p 074

PATTERN
27 parts

p 082

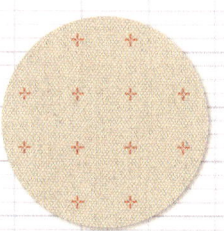

CLOTH
20 parts

p 090

PAPER
14 parts

p 100

PHOTO
34 parts

p 106

About the CD-ROM
p 110

flower01

flower02

flower03

flower04

flower05

flower06

flower07

flower08

flower09

flower10

flower11

flower12

flower13

flower14

flower15

flower16

008

The background material on this page is cloth02 (p 91).

flower17

flower18

flower19

flower20

flower21

flower22

flower23

flower24

flower25

flower26

flower27

flower28

flower29

flower30

flower31

flower32

flower33

flower34

flower35

flower36

flower37

010

flower38

flower39

flower40

flower41

flower42

green02

green03

green04

green05

green06

green01

green07

green08

green09

012

green10

green11

green12

green13

green14

green15

green16

green17

green18

green19

green20

green21

green22

green23

green24

green25

green26

green27

green28

green29

green30

048

green31

green32

green33

green34

green35

green36

green37

green38

green39

014

The ornaments on this page are animal11 (p 18).

green40

green41

green42

green43

green44

green45

green46

015

green48

green49

green47

green51

green50

green52

green53

green54

green55

016

green56

green57

green58

green59

sample green13 (p 12) + animal34 (p 20) + paper01 (p 100) + photo15 (p 107)

animal01

animal02

animal03

animal04

animal05

animal06

animal07

animal08

animal09

animal10

animal11

animal12

018

animal13

animal14

animal15

animal16

animal17

animal20

animal21

animal18

animal19

animal22

animal24

animal25

animal26

animal27

animal23

animal28

animal29

animal30

animal31

animal32

animal33

animal34

animal35

animal39

animal36

animal40

animal37

animal38

animal41

021

animal42

animal43

animal44

The ornaments on this page are goods07 (p 22), goods 45 (p 26).

goods01

goods02

goods03

goods06

goods04

goods05

goods07

goods08

goods09

goods10

goods11

goods13

goods14

goods12

goods18

goods17

goods16

goods15

goods21

goods20

goods19

023

goods22

goods23

goods24

sample animal14 (p 19) + ribbon19 (p 38) + ribbon20 (p 38) + flame46 (p 57) + type6 (p 68) + lace01 (p 70) + pattern07 (p 86) + paper09 (p 102)

goods25

goods26

goods28

goods29

goods27

goods30

goods34

goods36

goods31

goods33

goods35

025

goods37

goods38

goods32

goods39

goods40

goods41

goods42

goods43

goods44

goods45

goods46

goods47

goods48

goods49

goods50

goods51

goods52

goods53

026

green39 (p 14) + green43 (p 15) + green44 (p 15) + animal20 (p 19) + corner05 (p 44)

goods54

goods55

goods56

028

goods57   goods58   goods59   goods60

029

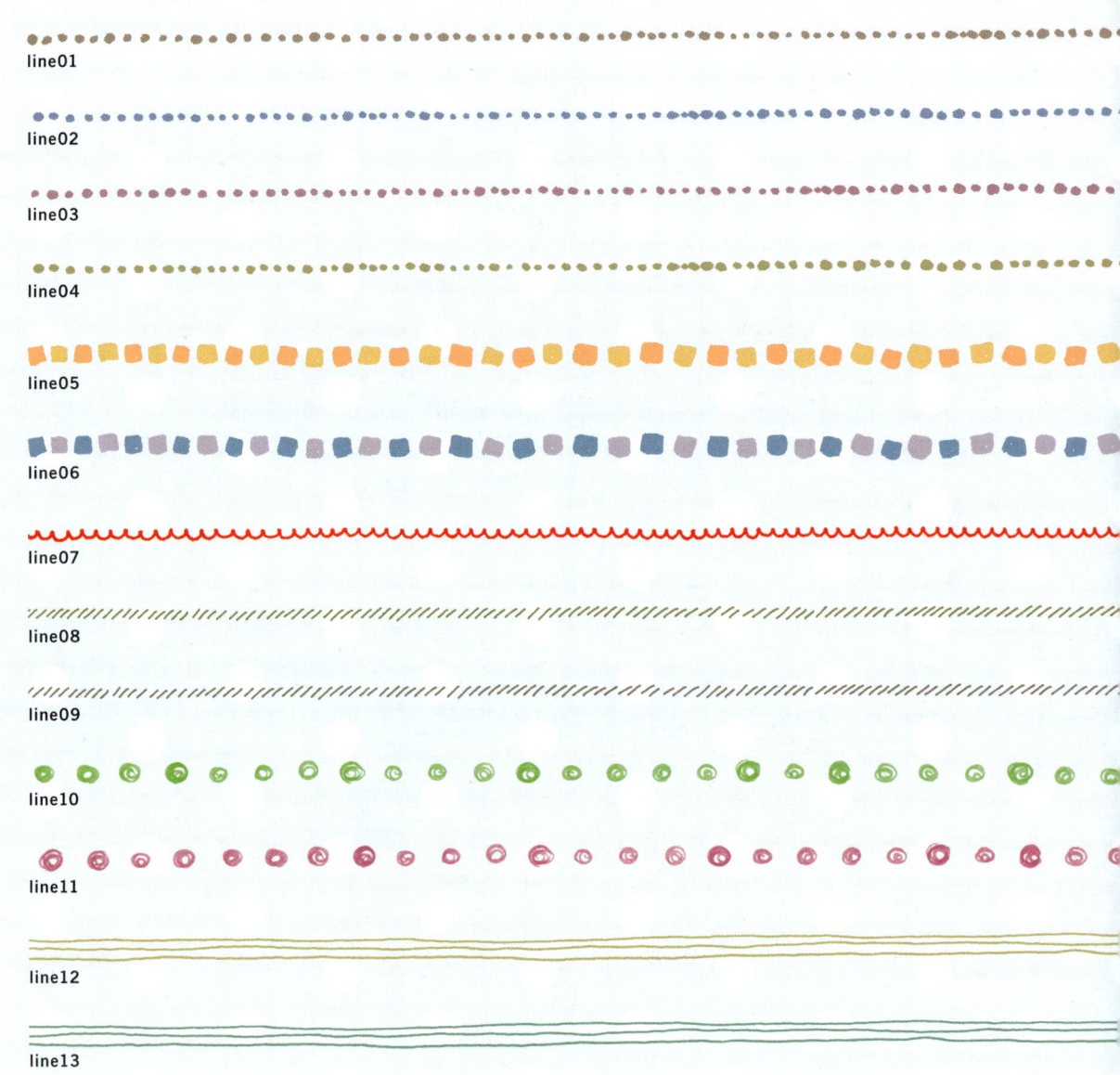

line01

line02

line03

line04

line05

line06

line07

line08

line09

line10

line11

line12

line13

030

The background material on this page is cloth15 (p 97).

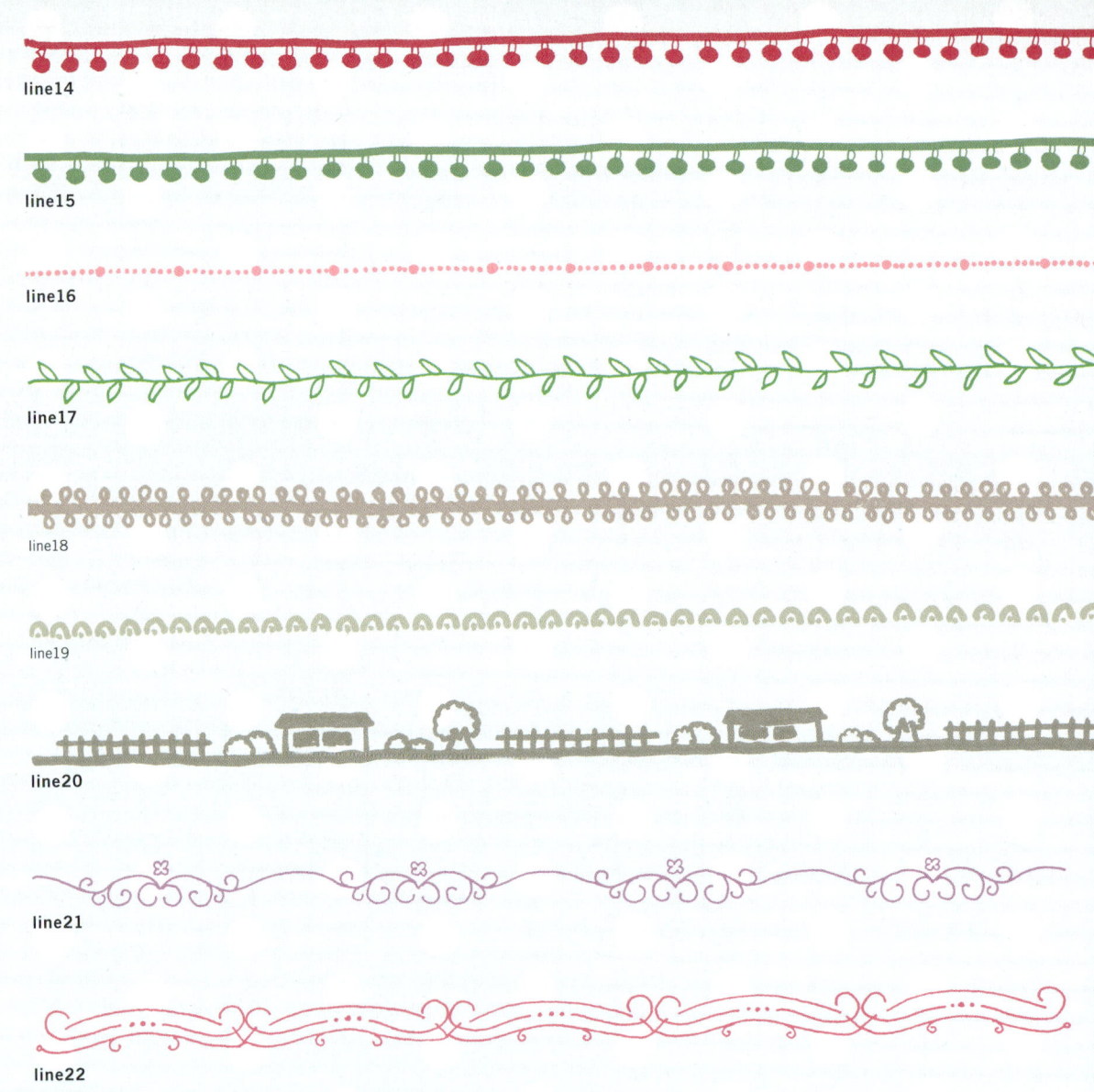

line14

line15

line16

line17

line18

032

line19

line20

line21

line22

line23

line24

033

line25

line26

line27

line28

line29

line30

line31

line32

ribbon01

ribbon02

ribbon03

ribbon04

ribbon08

ribbon09

ribbon10

The ornament materials on this page are animal036 (p 21) and goods01, 02, 03, 04 (p 22).

ribbon05

ribbon06

ribbon07

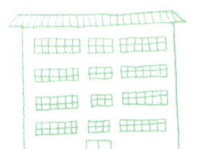

ribbon11

ribbon12

ribbon13

ribbon14

ribbon15

ribbon16

ribbon17

ribbon18

ribbon19

ribbon20

038

The ornament materials on this page are goods01, 02, 03, 04 (p 22) and goods051 (p 26).

ribbon21

ribbon22

ribbon23

ribbon24

ribbon25

ribbon26

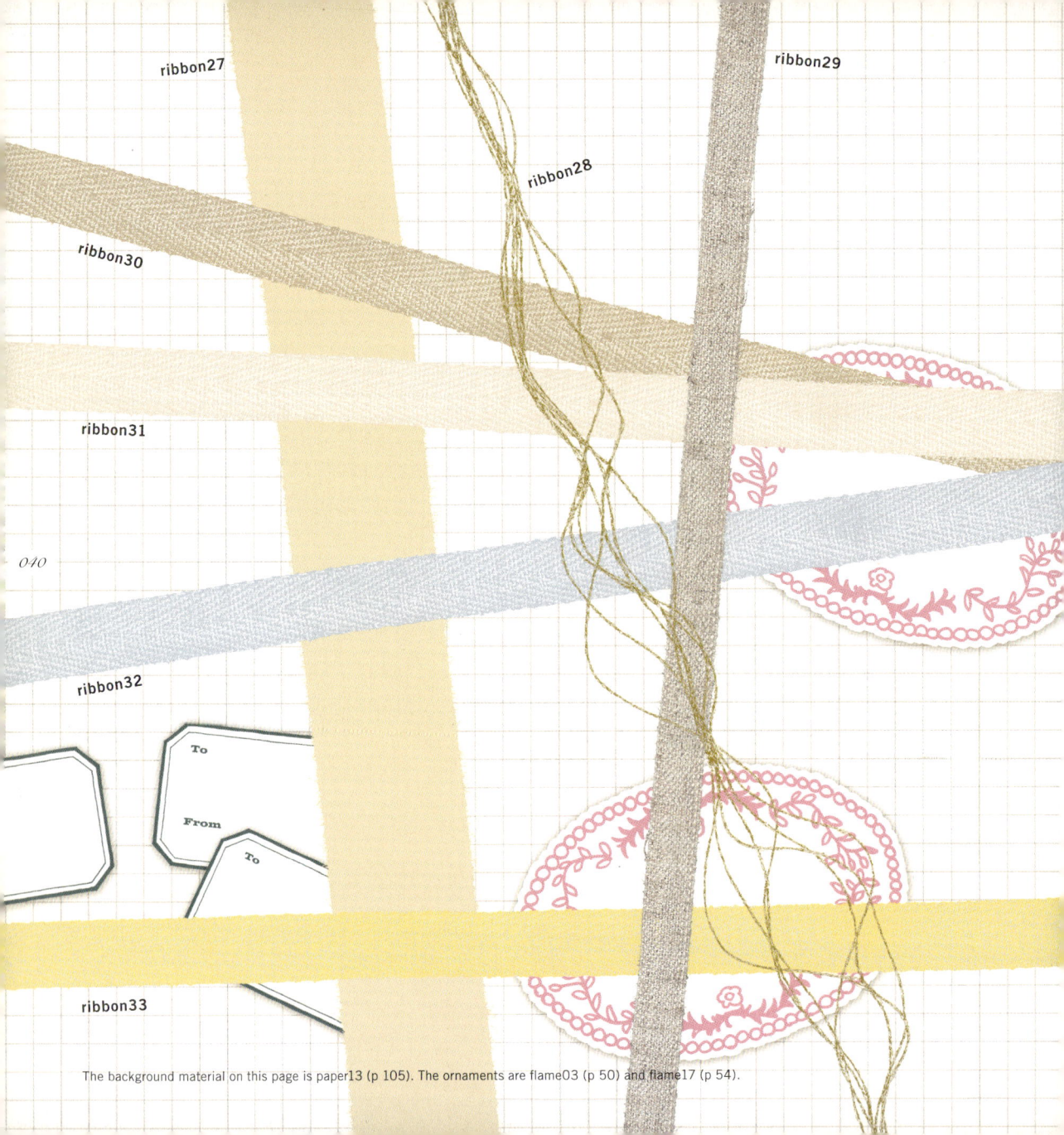

ribbon27

ribbon29

ribbon28

ribbon30

ribbon31

040

ribbon32

To

From

To

ribbon33

The background material on this page is paper13 (p 105). The ornaments are flame03 (p 50) and flame17 (p 54).

ribbon34

ribbon35

ribbon36

011

To

From

To

Fr

To

corner01_1

corner01_2

042

corner01_3

corner01_4

The background material on this page is paint02 (p 74).

corner02_1

corner02_2

corner02_3

corner02_4

043

corner03_1

corner03_2

corner04_1

corner04_2

corner03_3

corner03_4

corner04_3

corner04_4

corner05_1

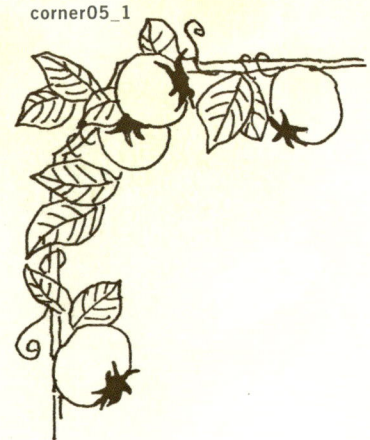

corner05_2

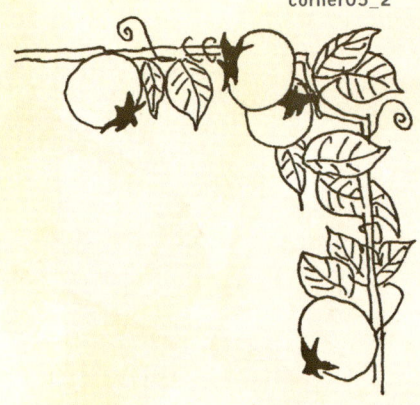

044

corner05_3

corner05_4

corner06_1

corner06_2

corner06_3

corner06_4

corner07_1

corner07_2

corner08_1

corner08_2

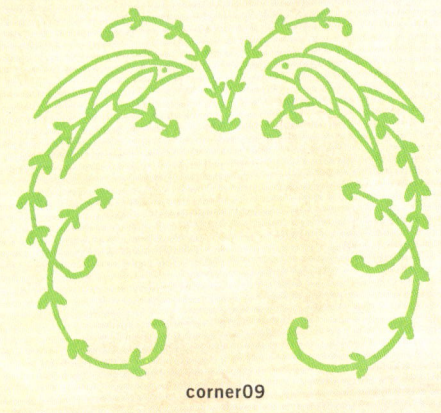

corner09

corner08_3

corner08_4

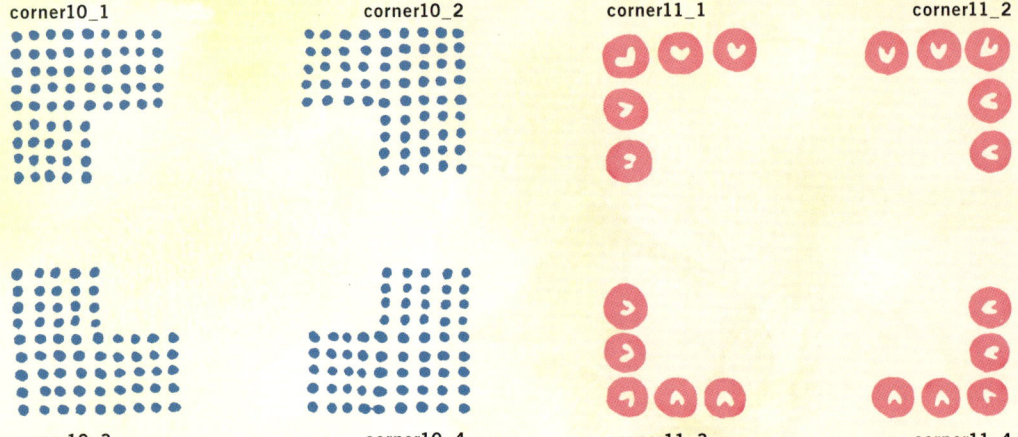

corner10_1

corner10_2

corner11_1

corner11_2

corner10_3

corner10_4

corner11_3

corner11_4

046

corner12_1

corner12_2

corner13_1

corner13_2

flower01 (p 8) + flower16 (p 8) + green09 (p 12) + animal10 (p 18) + line23 (p 33) + line24 (p 33) + paper12 (p 105)

corner14_1

corner14_2

corner15_1

corner15_2

corner17_1

corner16

corner17_2

corner18_1

corner18_2

corner19_1

corner19_2

018

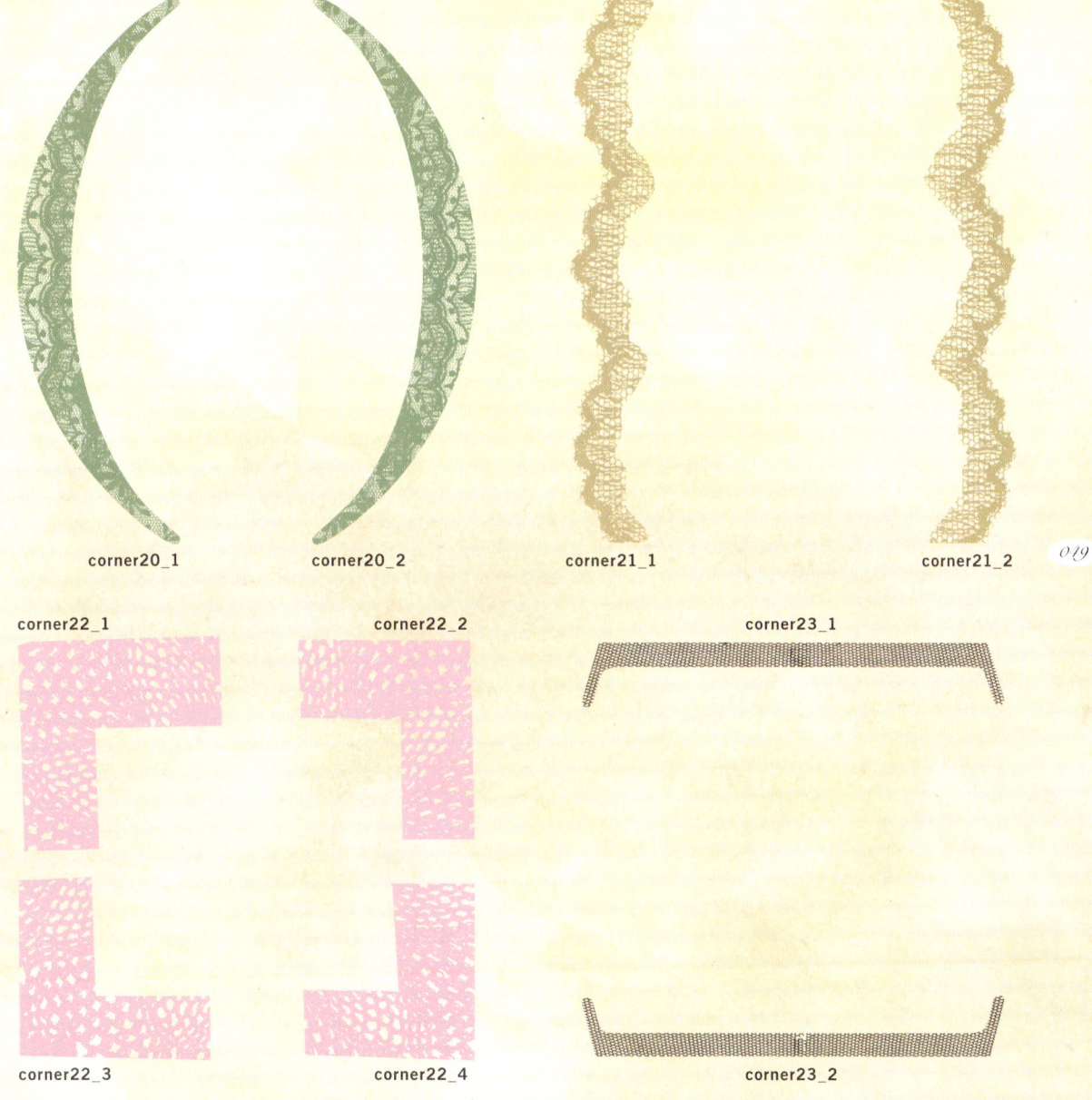

corner20_1

corner20_2

corner21_1

corner21_2

corner22_1

corner22_2

corner23_1

corner22_3

corner22_4

corner23_2

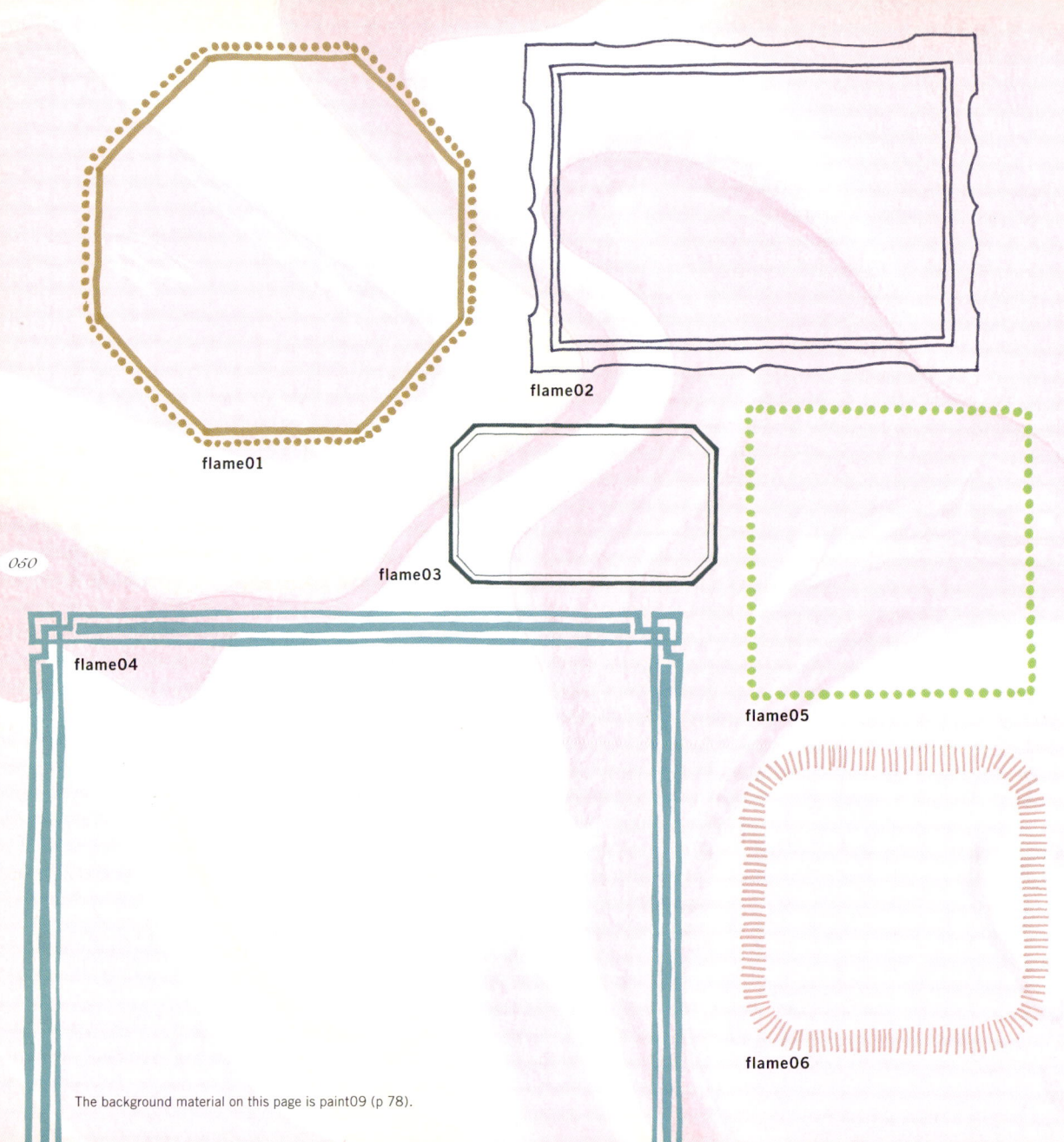

flame01

flame02

flame03

flame04

flame05

flame06

050

The background material on this page is paint09 (p 78).

flame07

flame08

flame09

flame10

flame11

flame12

051

flame13

flame14

flame15

flame16

flame17

flame18

flame19

054

flame20

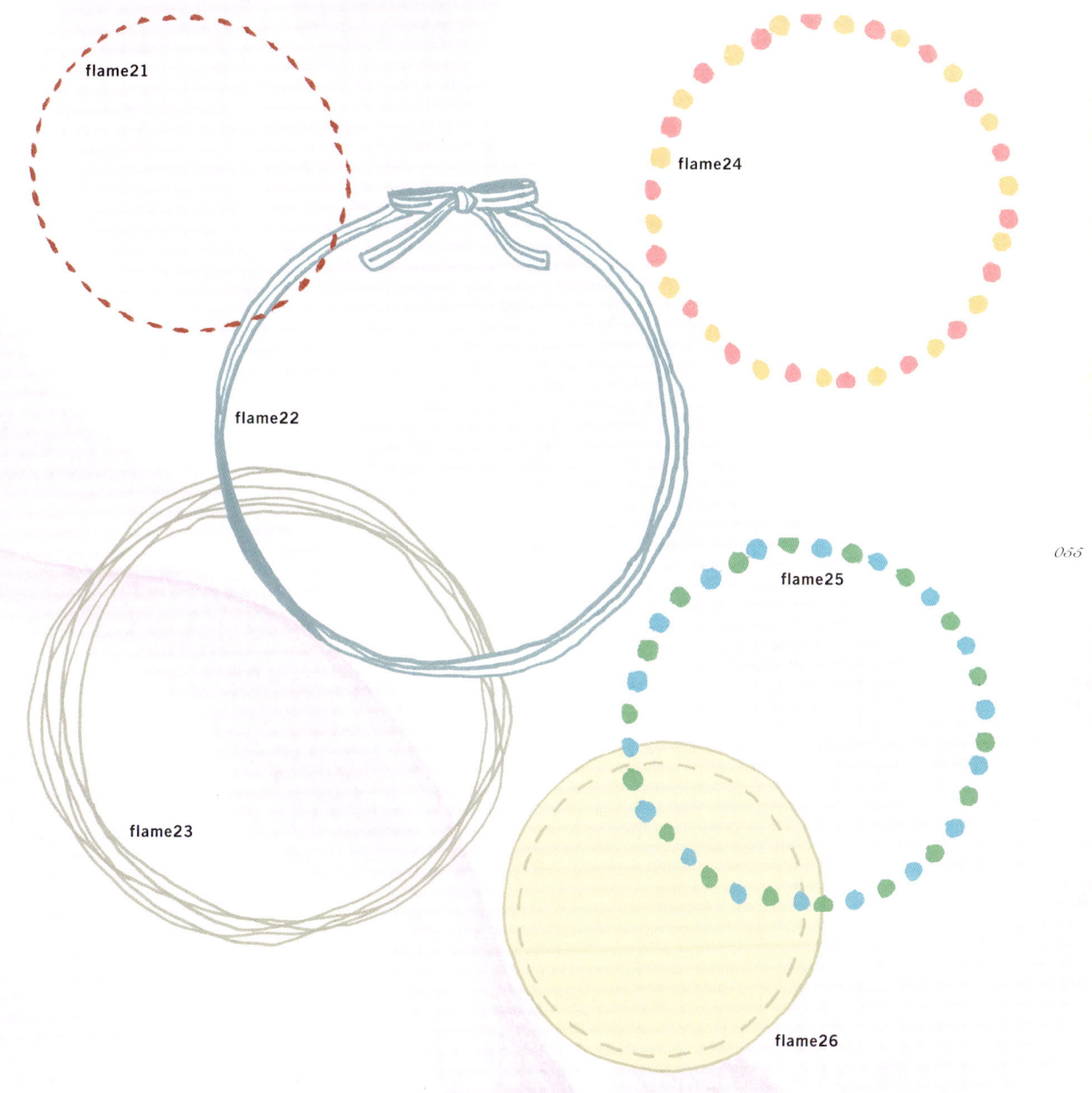

flame21

flame22

flame23

flame24

flame25

flame26

flame27

flame28

flame29

flame30

flame31

flame32

flame33

flame34

flame35

flame36

flame37

flame38

056

flame39

flame40

flame41

flame42

flame43

flame44

flame45

flame46

flame47

type1_B

type1_C

type1_D

type1_A

type1_I type1_J type1_K type1_L

type1_R type1_S type1_T type1_U type1_V

type1_Q

type1_Y type1_Z

type1_sign3

type1_sign1 type1_sign2

type1_sign4

type1_O type1_1 type1_2 type1_3 type1_4

The background material on this page is type1 (p 58).

type1_E　　type1_F　　type1_G　　type1_H

type1_M　　　　type1_N　　　　type1_O

type1_P

059

type1_W　　type1_X

type1_sign7

type1_

type1_sign8

type1_sign9

t y p e 1 _　type1_sign6

type1_5　　type1_6　　type1_7　　type1_8　　type1_9

flower10 (p 8) + animal10 (p 18) + animal38 (p 21) + goods54 (p 28) + goods59 (p 29) + flame16 (p 53) + paint15 (p 81)

type2_A
type2_B
type2_C
type2_D
type2_E
type2_F
type2_G
type2_H
type2_I
type2_J
type2_K
type2_L
type2_M
type2_N
type2_O
type2_P
type2_Q
type2_R
type2_S
type2_T
type2_U
type2_V
type2_W
type2_X
type2_Y
type2_Z
type2_sign1
type2_sign2
type2_sign3
type2_0
type2_1
type2_2
type2_3
type2_4
type2_5
type2_6
type2_7
type2_8
type2_9

061

The ornaments on this page are flower01 (p 8), flower42 (p 11), green56 (p 16), animal07 (p 18), animal36 (p 21) and goods16 (p 23).

type3_A   type3_B   type3_C   type3_D   type3_E

type3_J   type3_K   type3_L   type3_M

type3_R   type3_S   type3_T   type3_U

type3_Y   type3_Z   type3_sign1   type3_sign2   type3_sign3   type3_sign4

type3_0   type3_1   type3_2   type3_3   type3_4

062

The ornaments on this page are ribbon01 and ribbon03 (p 36).

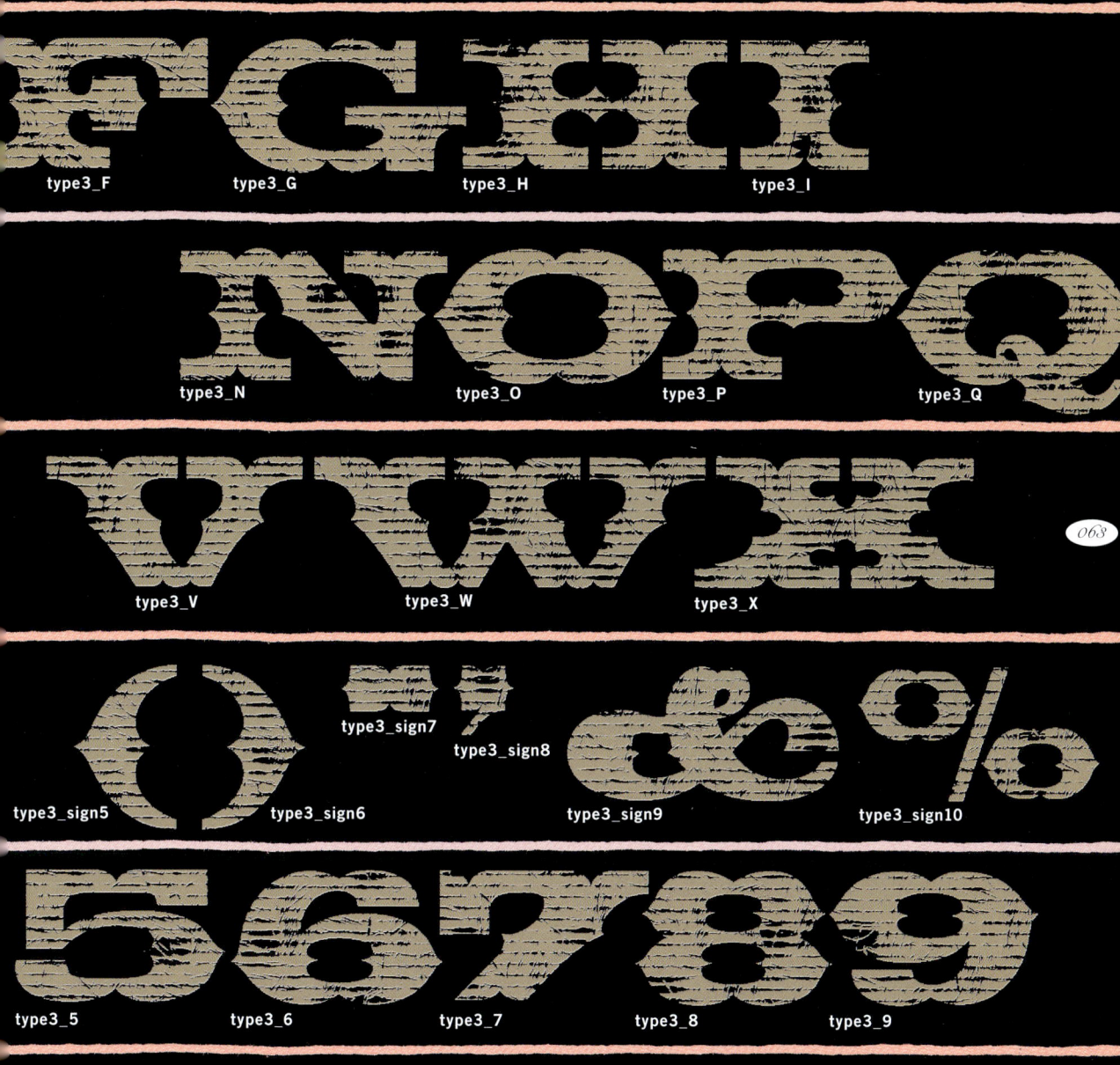

type3_F　　type3_G　　type3_H　　type3_I

type3_N　　type3_O　　type3_P　　type3_Q

type3_V　　type3_W　　type3_X

063

type3_sign7

type3_sign8

type3_sign5　　type3_sign6　　type3_sign9　　type3_sign10

type3_5　　type3_6　　type3_7　　type3_8　　type3_9

type4_A

type4_B

type4_C

type4_D

type4_K

type4_L

type4_M

type4_S

type4_T

type4_U

type4_V

type4_sign1 type4_sign2

type4_sign3

type4_0 type4_1 type4_2

The ornament on this page is line26 (p 34).

type4_E
type4_F
type4_G
type4_H
type4_I
type4_J
type4_N
type4_O
type4_P
type4_Q
type4_R
type4_W
type4_X
type4_Y
type4_Z
type4_6
type4_3
type4_4
type4_5
type4_7
type4_8
type4_9

type5_A type5_B type5_C type5_D type5_E type5_F type5_G

type5_H type5_I type5_J type5_K type5_L type5_M type5_N

type5_O type5_P type5_Q type5_R type5_S type5_T type5_U

type5_V type5_W type5_X type5_Y type5_Z

type5_sign1 type5_sign2 type5_sign3

type5_0 type5_1 type5_2 type5_3 type5_4 type5_5

type5_6 type5_7 type5_8 type5_9

The background material on this page is cloth06 (p 97).

sample | ribbon28 (p 40) + ribbon35 (p 41) +corner17 (p 48) + corner21 (p 49) + photo25 (p 108)

type6_A   type6_B   type6_C   type6_D   type6_E

type6_L   type6_M   type6_N   type6_O   type6_P

068

type6_V   type6_W   type6_X   type6_Y   type6_Z

type6_0   type6_1   type6_2

The background material on this page is cloth19 (p 99).

type6_F type6_G type6_H type6_I type6_J type6_K

type6_Q type6_R type6_S type6_T type6_U

069

type6_sign1 type6_sign2 type6_sign3

type6_3 type6_4 type6_5 type6_6 type6_7 type6_8 type6_9

lace01

lace02

lace03

The background material on this page is paper02 (p 101).

lace04

lace05

lace06

feather02

feather03

feather01

feather04

feather05

feather06

The background material on this page is flame19 (p 54).

feather07

feather08

feather09

feather10

feather11

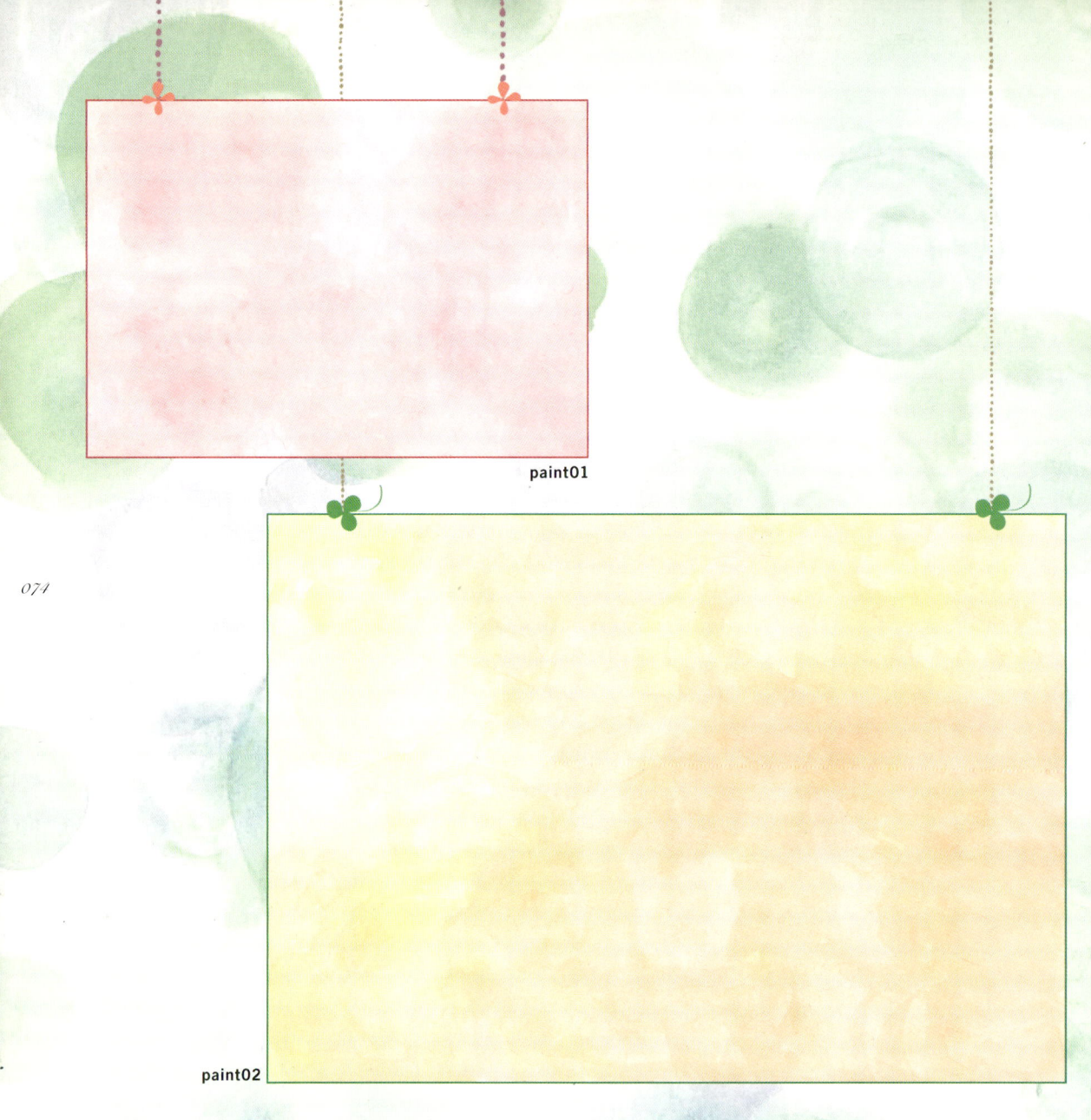

paint01

paint02

The background material on this page is paint07 (p 76). The ornaments are flower06 (p 8), green20 (p 13), goods39 (p 26) and line02, 03, 04 (p 30).

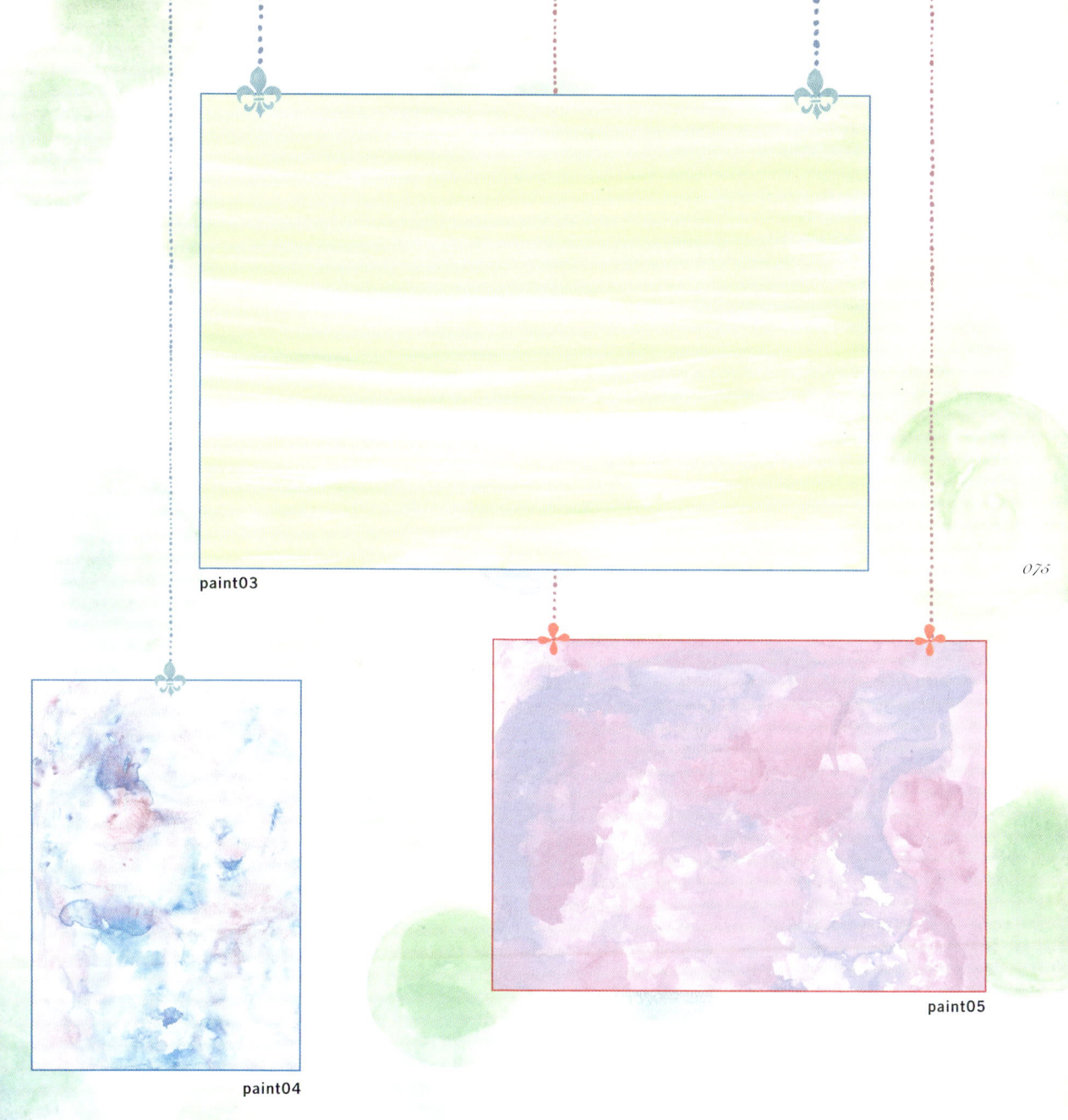

paint03

paint04

paint05

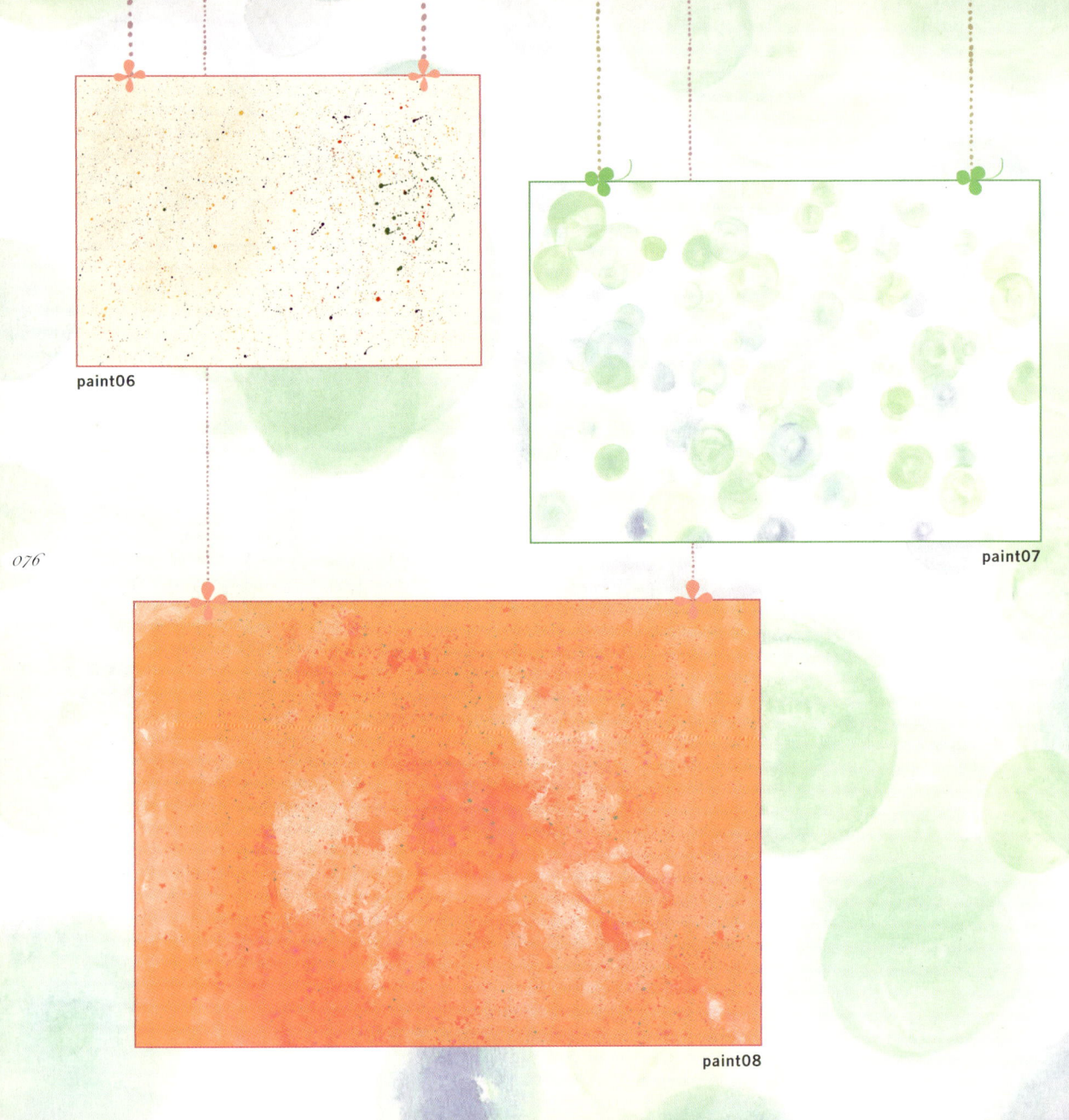

paint06

paint07

paint08

MOON

SUN

CANDLE

sample goods49 (p 26) + goods51 (p 26) + goods53 (p 26) + paper06 (p 102) + paper10 (p 104)

paint09

paint10

paint11

paint12

paint13

080

paint14

paint15

paint16

pattern01

The background material on this page is cloth14 (p 97). The ornaments are flower06 (p 8), green20 (p 13), goods39 (p 26) and line02, 03, 04 (p 30).

pattern02

pattern03

pattern04

sample green45 (p 15) + green47 (p 16) + animal21 (p 19) + line07 (p 30) + paint01 (p 74) + paint03 (p 75) + paint08 (p 76)+ pattern25 (p 89) + cloth01 (p 90).

pattern06

pattern05

085

086

pattern07

pattern08

pattern09

pattern10

pattern11

pattern12

pattern13

pattern14

pattern15

pattern16

pattern17

pattern18

088

The background material on this page is cloth02 (p 91).

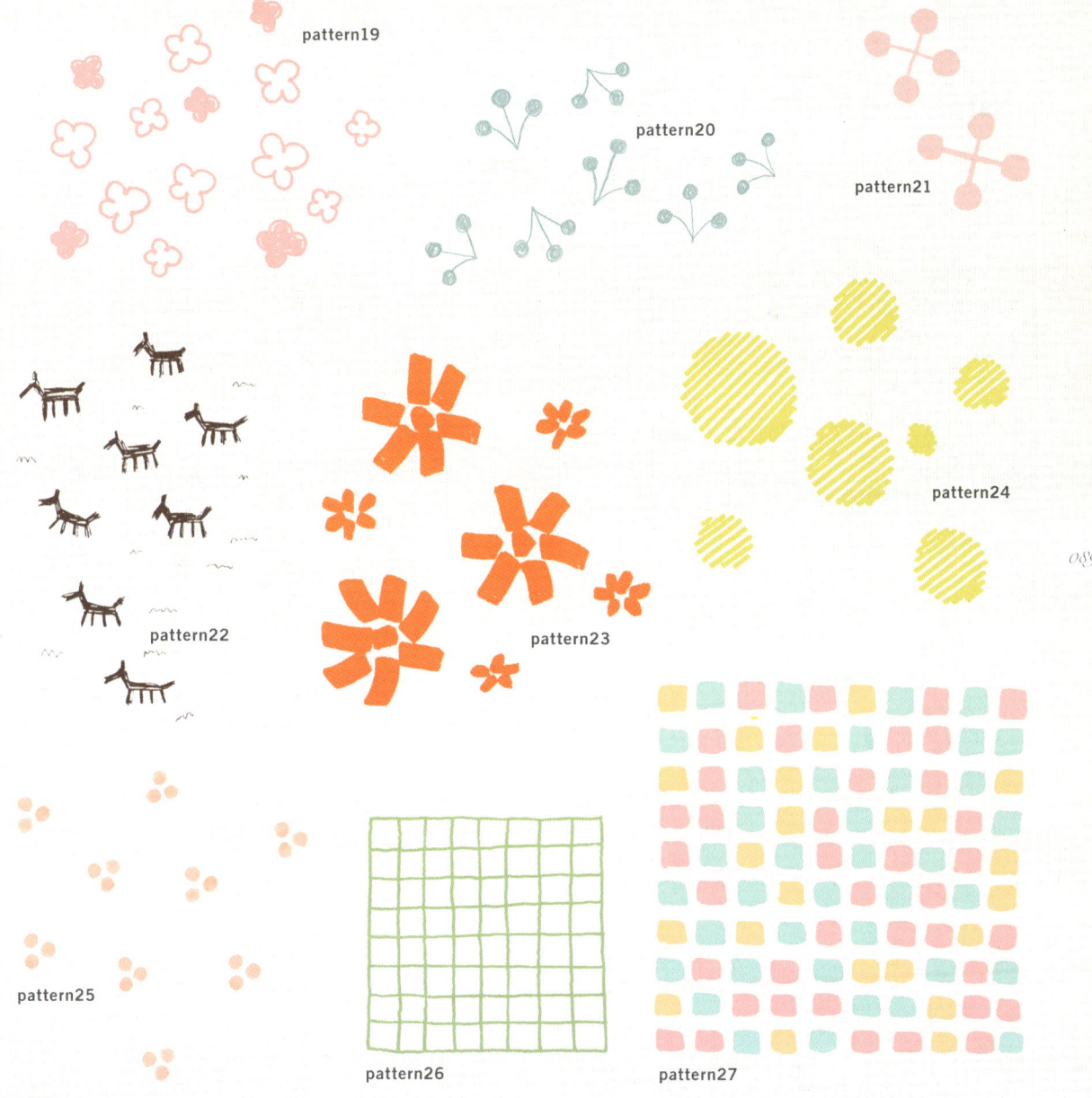

pattern19

pattern20

pattern21

pattern22

pattern23

pattern24

pattern25

pattern26

pattern27

089

The images on these pages are enlarged parts of cloth materials.

cloth01

The background material on this page is animal02 (p 18). The ornament is line02 (p 30).

cloth02

cloth03

891

cloth04

cloth05

cloth06

cloth07

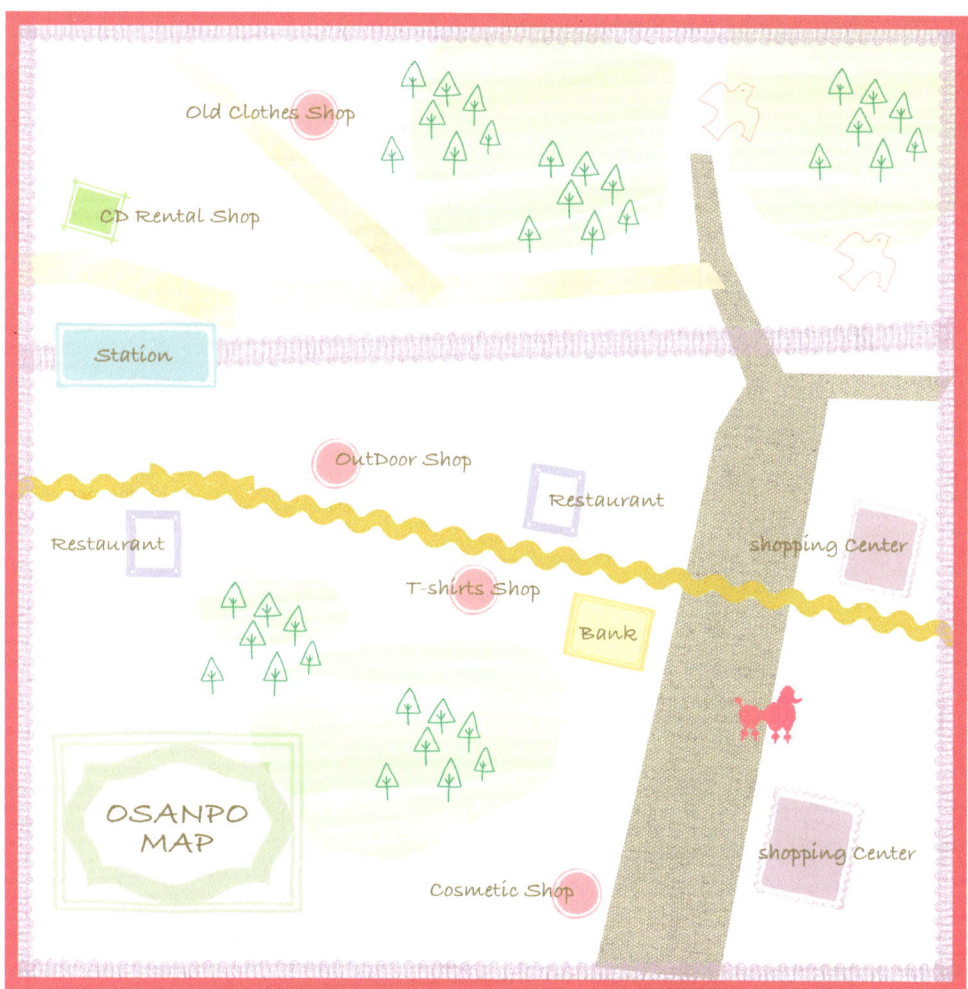

Old Clothes Shop

CD Rental Shop

Station

OutDoor Shop

Restaurant

Restaurant

T-shirts Shop

Bank

shopping Center

OSANPO MAP

Cosmetic Shop

shopping Center

sample | animal07 (p 18) + animal25 (p 20) + ribbon21 (p 39) + ribbon25 (p 39) + flame27 (p 56) + flame28 (p 56) + flame29 (p 56) + flame31 (p 56) + flame32 (p 56) + flame37 (p 56) + flame38 (p 56) + paint02 (p 74) + paint03 (p 75) + pattern17 (p 88) + cloth07 (p 92)

cloth08

cloth09

cloth10

cloth11

cloth12

cloth13

cloth14

cloth15

cloth16

cloth17

cloth18

cloth19

cloth20

The images on these pages are enlarged parts of paper materials.

paper01

The background material on this page is lace02 (p 70) and lace05, 06 (p 71). The ornament is flame32 (p 56).

paper02

paper03

paper04

paper05

paper06

paper07

paper08

paper09

sample　flower36 (p 10) + flower40 (p 11) + line01 (p 30) + line29 (p 34)

paper11

paper12

paper13

paper14

photo01

photo02

photo03

photo04

106

photo05

photo06

photo07

photo08

photo09

The background material on this page is cloth01 (p 90). The ornaments are corner01 (p 42), corner03, 04 (p 43) and corner17 (p 48).

photo10

photo11

photo12

photo13

photo14

photo15

photo16

photo17

photo18

photo19

photo20

photo21

108

photo22

photo23

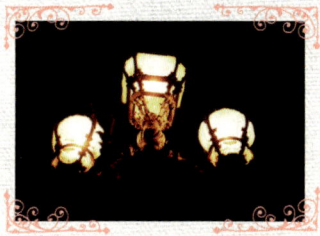

photo24

photo25

photo26

photo27

photo28

photo29

photo30

photo31

photo32

photo33

photo34

ABOUT THE CD-ROM

About the files

The files are all saved as RGB mode, JPEG files with a resolution of 350dpi. Elements without backgrounds in the book, such as illustration parts, are saved as JPEG files and PNG files (with transparent backgrounds).

JPEG
JPEG (.jpg) is a file format that works with most image-editing applications. Backgrounds appear as white areas.

PNG
PNG (.png) is a file format that features a transparent background. It is suitable for creating layered images. PNG files can be imported into image-processing software. Textured materials, which do not require transparent backgrounds, only appear as JPEGs.

Some versions of image-editing software do not recognize JPEG or PNG files. Please check the software's instruction manual beforehand.

The files have been designated as "read-only" to avoid unintentional overwriting. Therefore, when you copy the file from the CD-ROM and use it on your computer the newly processed and retouched materials will not be saved in the original file. In that case, users must remove the "read-only" designation, or rename the files when saving them.

About colors

When printing files, please note that there may be a slight difference between the colors of the images when they appear in the book and when they appear on your computer monitor.

About licensing

Purchasers, regardless if they are individuals or corporations (for commercial use), may use and re-create freely the materials on this CD-ROM. There is no need for licensing or credits. Therefore, there is no need to pay copyright fees or royalties. In addition, designs can be used worldwide, as there is no regional limits of use.

However, unauthorized reproduction, transfer, distribution, or selling of the data or infringement of the copyright is prohibited. All rights about the contents of this book and CD-ROM are reserved to the publisher.

Examples of unauthorized uses:
1. Sales of the material data, editing in CD-ROM, and other media
2. Trademark registration or production of characterized goods of the images of data
3. Showing the data on the Web, or making them downloadable
4. Production and sales of goods that include contents of the data

About the size (and resolution) of files

The image files have a resolution of 350 dpi, which suits commercial printing.

Here are some samples to show you the sizes of materials.

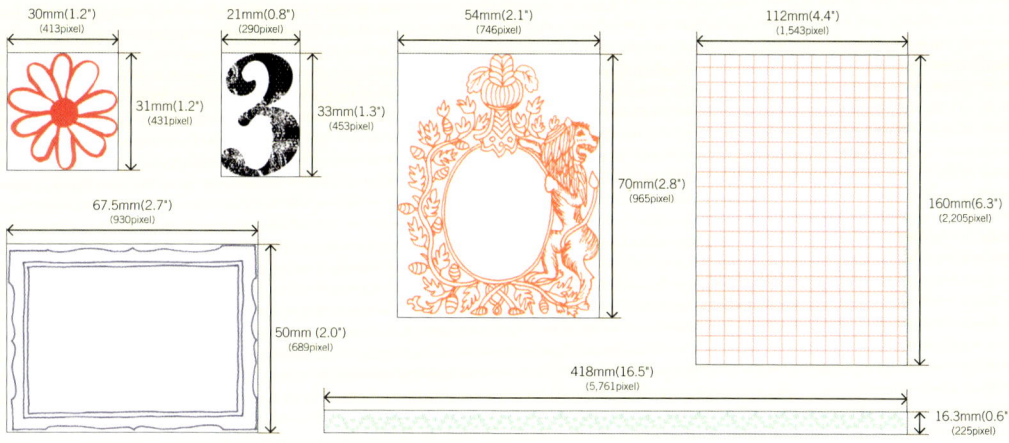

30mm(1.2")
(413pixel)

31mm(1.2")
(431pixel)

21mm(0.8")
(290pixel)

33mm(1.3")
(453pixel)

54mm(2.1")
(746pixel)

70mm(2.8")
(965pixel)

112mm(4.4")
(1,543pixel)

160mm(6.3")
(2,205pixel)

67.5mm(2.7")
(930pixel)

50mm (2.0")
(689pixel)

418mm(16.5")
(5,761pixel)

16.3mm(0.6")
(225pixel)